Barbara Miller

How to Write a Book and Tell Your Story

Easy Steps to Write, Publish, and Promote Your Book

Enrich lives through the stories you tell!

2014 Barbara & Company International, Inc. Trade Paperback Edition
Copyright © 2014 by Barbara Miller

All rights reserved. No part of this publication may be reproduced, stored in a retrieval system, or transmitted, in any form or by any means, electronic, mechanical, photocopying, recording, or otherwise, without the written prior permission of the author. The reader understands that contents of this book is not a guarantee to their personal success as a writer. This book was written for entertainment purposes.

Published in the United States by Barbara & Company International, Inc.

ISBN: 0988185245
ISBN 978-0-9881852-4-1
Library of Congress Control Number: 2014912859
Barbara & Company Int'l, Incorporated, Naples, FL

ATTENTION CORPORATIONS, UNIVERSITIES, COLLEGES, and PROFESSIONAL ORGANIZATIONS: Quantity discounts are available on bulk purchases of this book for educational, gift purposes, or as premiums for increasing magazine subscriptions or renewals. Special books or book excerpts can also be created to fit specific needs.
Printed in the United States of America
www.barbaraandcompany.com

DEDICATION

This book is dedicated to my new wonderful friend and life coach June Kellogg. She is a beautiful sparkling diamond sent by the Universe just when I needed her.

ACKNOWLEDGEMENTS

I am so blessed to have a wonderful supportive husband who graciously read my manuscript more times than he wanted to. He is my rock and I am so thankful for his encouragement, and yes his feedback, even if we disagreed. Often times he is right! I love and appreciate you my amazing David, from the bottom of my heart.

TABLE OF CONTENTS

Chapter 1 .... Why Write a Book?   1
81% of people say they want to write a book. Be one of the 2% who actually do it. Learn easy steps to propel you to take action.

Chapter 2 .... What Should I Write About?   9
Write what you know and are excited about. Glean information to help you zero in on your topic. Learn how to write to your audience.

Chapter 3 .... Research Research Research   19
Read others author's work. How to research your topic and put it in your own words. Learn the value in knowing your subject. Make Google and Amazon your friends.

Chapter 4 .... Choosing a Publisher   25
Explore your choices—vanity, traditional, or self-publish. How to make the best choice and create a plan of action.

Chapter 5 .... Start at the Beginning   33
See the worth of an outline in a few easy steps. Learn how to organize your research material and stay true to your topic. Easy techniques to avoid writer's block.

Chapter 6 .... Let's Rough It   41
Write like you speak, not like a college term paper. Let your words flow freely and watch your story give birth without labor pains.

Chapter 7 .... Now Let's Publish Your Book   49
Publish with ease through Amazon's Create Space or Kindle Direct Publishing. See how easy—breezy it is to publish through these two platforms. Amazon continues to make it easy for newbie authors to publish their books.

Chapter 8.............Create a Show Stopping Cover   55
Experience the value of 'shopping around' for bargains. Fiverr and eLance to the rescue. Make a statement through the 'Dynamic Trio,' *title, cover, back cover copy.*

Chapter 9.............How to Promote Your Book   63
Give your book a showcase and let it shine. It needs a special home to do this and that of course is your website and blog. Easy steps to have your website and blog up and running in 24 hours, cheaper than a Starbucks Latté.

Chapter 10...........Let's Socialize   71
Learn the value in blogging, socializing, and how to create interest in your book. Pin it, Tweet it, Face it, Like it, Link it, and make it a Good Read, and in other words, help them to know, like, and trust you. Let them help you sell your books.

Chapter 11............Okay I'm Immortal—Now What   79
How to release the news with a press release, actually 3 press releases. Get those reviews to help sell your book. Let Amazon promote you FREE, through your Author Page. Enlist your friends to help with reviews. Enlist the troops—Fiverr, Amazon, Facebook, Twitter, LinkedIn, Pinterest, Goodread's.

"Twenty years from now you will be more disappointed by the things that you didn't do than by the ones you did do. So throw off the bowlines. Sail away from the safe harbor. Catch the trade winds in your sails. Explore. Dream. Discover."—Mark Twain

INTRODUCTION

Why I Wrote This Book

I want to help you become one of the 2% who actually write their book, instead of the 81% who say they have a book in them but never write it. I have had a love affair with books from the time I was a little girl. Books to me were magical as they transported me to a make-believe world of places, characters, and fantasies.

I grew up on stories told by my mother and grandmother. I want my readers to know how easy it can be to tell your own stories, and capture the reader's attention, as you draw them into your inner world of thoughts and characters, brought to life by your words. When strung together properly, your stories could hold them captive for hours on end.

This book will take the mystery out of the process of writing your own book. The world needs your stories that only you could present in your own voice—words.

I still use the same steps to write, publish, and promote my books as you will read about on these pages. It is my desire that you open your inner door and let the words flow out for the world to read. What are you waiting for? Grab a pen and notebook or open a Word doc on your computer and begin. We are waiting for you!

WHAT THIS BOOK IS ABOUT

This book is about the process of teaching you how to share your stories. How to Write a Book and Tell Your Story, is directed at the 'newbie author' to help take overwhelm out of writing your book. I have laid out simple steps, from choosing the subject to the actual writing process, and all the steps in between. Writing a book does not have to be hard. Sticking with it is the hard part. This book will help you stay on target and reach your goal, which is seeing your name in print!

The digital world has made it easy for anyone to find information on practically any subject known to man. Make this book your blueprint as you go through the book writing process with a system in place to keep you on track. Learn how to get your book edited for as little as five dollars! There are valuable tips to help you stay the distance and reach the mark.

I explain how you can even get your book published without spending a dime. You will also learn the best and most efficient method to publish your book. I have also included ways to promote and get your book in the hands of readers. I will show you how to use social media to promote your book and get your name in front of millions.

You will quickly learn how to get your book up on Amazon with ease. Use Amazon's Create Space and Kindle Direct Publishing to help you bring your book to print. Amazon is a powerhouse, selling 65% of all digital books!

Writing your book is a splendid journey with an amazing destination—your book in print! Whether you are writing your own life story, mystery, romance, genealogy, health and wellness, a cookbook, your hobby—tell your story.

Chapter 1
WHY WRITE A BOOK?

"I want to do something splendid...Something heroic or wonderful that won't be forgotten after I'm dead...I think I shall write books."—Louisa May Alcott

See Your Name in Print

Many people want to write a book. There is something magical about seeing your work and your name in print. However, most will only imagine it in their mind, and few will put words on paper. Why do you want to write a book and what is your goal once your book is finished? What do you want your book to do for you? I wanted to use my book as a tool for speaking engagements, seminars, and life coaching. Having a goal in place will help you stay focused and working towards achieving your goal. I believed I needed to write my book in order to create credibility and trust to promote myself as a qualified seminar leader, speaker, and coach. That was the driving force for completing my books.

We Love Our Books

There is something I find amazing about books. People rarely part with them and usually display them in a prominent place: a bookshelf, a coffee table, or a nightstand. We love our books and if someone dares to borrow one, they darn sure better remember to give it back, because we do not forget. I recently had a woman I used to work with hand me a book she had borrowed five years earlier. She said, "Oh, I was sorting through some things and came across this book I borrowed from you and thought you might like it back." Yeah, I wanted it back years ago! People all over the world love books, and they treat authors like the authorities they are. Everyone would like to write a book, but only a few will have a burning desire and discipline to complete and publish a book and hold it in their hands. You can be one of the few respected authors who can say, "I finally finished my book!"

Writing to Your Audience

What would you like your book to do for your reader? Do you want it to entertain, promote deep thinking, support a cause, or suggest the need for change? Whatever you want your book to accomplish will have to be decided before you begin to write. Establish who you want to write for and what genre you will choose;

Why Write a Book?

children's books, romance, crime, adventure, fantasy, horror, health and wellness, genealogy, comedy, are some of the choices. Will you write fiction or non-fiction? Many new writers have the idea that they write for themselves, and that is an incorrect assumption. If you want to sell your book, it must solve a problem or meet a need that the buyer is looking for. Writing to your audience is what you must accomplish in order to connect with potential readers who have only one goal in buying your book. Understanding this goal is paramount to selling your books. Here it is in a nutshell, WIIFM, "What's in it for me?" If your book does not answer this question, they will likely pass and purchase a book that offers what they need. Don't be preachy, as the reader will feel talked down to. People buy books emotionally, just like they buy cars and houses, and they must be able to *feel* the value.

81% Want to Write a Book

According to an article in the New York Times, 81% of people want to write a book. However, sadly, only about 2% will actually write their book. Which percent will you fall into, the 81% who say they have a book in them or the 2% who get the job done? Think about all of the information or history you have to offer the world that could be lost. All you need to write your book is a computer and some research. The reason your computer is so important is that in order to upload your book to Amazon, you will need to do it from a computer. Also, I have never met any editor I have used, or book cover designer, because it was all done online. You will also need your computer in order to have an author website and email. You certainly want book fans to be able to communicate with you. The investment in your new job as a writer is peanuts compared to the rewards of holding that published book in your hands.

One of the most common excuses I hear from those who say they have a book in them is "I just do not have time to write because I work fulltime." You can get started like I did while still holding down a fulltime job, and making the effort to get up early and spend at least one hour working on your book. In other words, you do not have to quit your *day job*, but you do have to make a commitment to keep your appointment with yourself each day to write your book. When you consider how much time is wasted sitting in traffic, doctor appointments, and on airplanes, you could use these blocks of time to record or write your thoughts. I have a small voice activated recorder that I keep in my car so I can record thoughts while sitting in traffic.

What Motivates You

What do you want to accomplish with your book? How do you plan to use it and what purpose will it serve? Have you considered your personal goals and written them down? Thinking about your goals is indeed the first step, but outlining them with pen and paper breathes more life into them. It is like starting to build a house. First we envision exactly what we want our home to look like, and then we sketch up a plan. We work the plan until it rings true to what we want in our new home, and then we have blueprints drawn up, and assuming we have secured the lot, we start the building project. We follow the building progress every day until we are finally gazing at our new home.

Take Action

This is exactly how our goals progress to reality, by taking action to build our dreams. If we do not take necessary steps towards our goals, our mind does not take us seriously. I hear this story frequently, "I always wanted to write a book, but I just could never find the time." When I ask them about their outline, they say, "Oh, that's all in my head." Well guess what, that is where it will likely stay. Wishing will not produce a written manuscript, and without a burning desire to hold that book in your hand, it will never happen! Our actions are reflected by what we believe. If you believe you can accomplish your goals, and physically move towards them, you will succeed! Only you can determine your motivation to reach your goals.

It's Your Time

I was having lunch one day with a group of women and one in particular asked me what I did for a living. I replied that I was writing a book. She turned her head to the side and rolled her eyes. Her actions were obvious to her thoughts which were— please give me a break; everybody is going to write a book. I was so embarrassed from her demoralizing look. Don't let people undermine your plans. Her attitude just fueled my determination to hold my book and personally place it in her hands. Which I did! The one thing I knew for sure was that I was writing a book, not that I was thinking about writing a book. She could not look inside my brain and see my goals and dreams, but it didn't change the fact that they were there. No one can totally understand you—but you. You are the one in charge of your future, so don't allow anyone else to take over that role. Your life dance belongs to you and only you! Sinclair Lewis said the right words, *"It is impossible to discourage the real writers—they don't give a damn what you say, they're going to write."*

Another example is while visiting with a friend one day and sharing my goals and dreams, I noticed that she remained silent and started looking down. Finally, she said, "Barbara, everyone would like to accomplish goals, but most never write a book. It is extremely difficult to write and promote a book. Are you certain you want to devote the time and effort it would take for such a lofty goal?" I was stunned and disappointed at her unwillingness to support and encourage me, and I will confess,

Why Write a Book?

her negative words and behavior hurt me deeply. However, I had learned a lot from Napoleon Hill, author of "Think and Grow Rich." I had clearly defined goals and definiteness of purpose. I was on a mission and I knew absolutely that I would write my book!

Stand in Your Power

Don't let people snatch away your power by *zapping* you. We have all been zapped at some point. You know the feeling when you are chatting and sharing and the person hits you in the gut with her mean spirited remark. You sit there stunned by her poison arrow zap, and she goes on without missing a beat. This is not a person who is loving and gracious and you may want to consider giving her your own zap—called the disappearing zap of your magic wand.

I have always known that I would write books eventually, but sometimes we have to put leverage on ourselves to keep us on track. I started to share with friends and clients that I was working on a book and intended to do public speaking and motivational seminars. There was no way I could let all of these different people down. Rarely did a week go by without someone asking, "So Barbara, how is that book coming?" Some days I wished I would have kept my mouth shut about the project, because then I would only be accountable to myself. Now I was accountable to others and I felt responsible to deliver what I had promised.

Be Prepared

I was always prepared to write by carrying a notepad and pen in my purse or beach bag, so whenever thoughts flashed into my mind, I was able to grab them and write them down. Great thoughts need to be recorded at once, as they may never grace your mind again, like the title I lost while out walking. As hard as I tried to recapture the thought, it was gone and I could not bring it back. So be prepared. Consider what you could do to change your current behavior to bring you one step closer to realizing your dreams. I used to get up at 5:00 a.m. to write before getting ready for work. I just kept reminding myself that I wanted a new career and it was writing books and public speaking. I believed my book was the catalyst that would help bring it all together. It never would have happened had I not had a burning desire to hold my printed book in my hands. It inspired me to keep writing and reading with profound passion!

Time to Begin

It is a fun escape for me to read a gripping thriller novel, but it is rare, as I love self-help books and have a library full of them. There are just as many people who love novels and never read self-help books. The point is that people need your ideas and books to enhance their lives, so don't let another day go by without starting your book. We have never had such opportunities available to us as we have today. Remember, the time is going to pass anyway. If you have started a book and it is sitting in mothballs, drag it out—dust it off and finish it! There is no perfect time to write your book, so pick up your pen or sit down in front of your computer and begin!

"Reinvent yourself, and you'll experience more added joy and contentment than you can imagine. A second act doesn't just change the specific aspect of your life that you're reinventing; it invigorates your entire life." —Stephen M. Pollen and Mark Levine, Second Acts

Why Write a Book?

Is there a book in you just screaming to get out?

___

___

___

___

___

___

___

___

Can you envision others reading your book?

___

___

___

___

___

___

___

___

What steps can you take today to start creating your book?

_____
_____
_____
_____
_____
_____
_____
_____

What does your book have to offer that will enrich or challenge others?

_____
_____
_____
_____
_____
_____
_____
_____

Why Write a Book?

How will you feel ten years from now if you never write your book?

_____
_____
_____
_____
_____
_____
_____
_____

Have you considered steps you might take to create time for writing your book?

_____
_____
_____
_____
_____
_____
_____
_____

Chapter 2
WHAT SHOULD I WRITE ABOUT?

"If you can tell stories, create characters, devise incidents, and have sincerity and passion, it doesn't matter a damn how you write."—
Somerset Maugham

What Blows Your Hair Back

You have heard this old cliché, but it is worth repeating, *write what you know.* What is it that you find interesting? As my old friend, known as Grandma Janet, used to say, "Well darling, now that really blows my hair back!" What blows your hair back? Maybe you already have a topic of interest that has been spinning around in your head. What could you write about that would be interesting for others to read? What are your passions? Whether you are an academic or a history buff or love chess—what gets your creative juices flowing?

Perhaps you keep a journal or diary and have notes from the last thirty years. Maybe you don't necessarily want the whole world to know your secrets and will choose to write under a pseudonym. Do you love steamy romance novels or does mystery blow your hair back? What books do you love to read? What draws you to a particular topic? What books are on your own bookshelf? You may have had life experiences that would interest others, like your attempt to navigate the world in your homemade sail boat. This could be turned into a thriller novel.

How about cooking and creating your own cookbook with recipes that you or your family have personally created? You might be a health and wellness guru, so consider a book on diet and exercise. Make it a book on how to enjoy cruise ship cuisine and not expand your waist line. Another great topic is to tell your travel stories and all the various exotic ports you have visited. People love travel books, especially if it is a place they would like to visit. How about writing a mystery that took place on a cruise ship? Be creative in your descriptions and draw your reader in so they can envision being on the trip with you.

What Should I Write About?

Tell Your Stories

Everyone loves to hear stories and writing really is the art of storytelling. Even little children beg us to tell them a story, which is exactly what happens in children's Sunday school programs at church. Imagine you are sitting around the campfire and sharing stories with friends or family. My mother used to sit with us in the evenings and read stories and nursery rhymes. I just loved it! I actually learned all those old nursery rhymes from my mother and can still quote many of them by heart. In fact, I taught them to my daughter, who now has children of her own. Stories have history. Do you remember the beautiful movie *"The English Patient?"* I especially loved the campfire scene, where they all took turns telling stories. Even the Bible was written from stories passed down through the generations. Telling stories is a way of life for all humans. Now put those stories down on paper. This is how books are born!

Perhaps you are a stock broker and would love to provide direction and pitfalls of investing your hard earned dollars. Maybe you have a unique method to help people create wealth and a book would give you credibility and recognition. If the internet is your forte, you may want to instruct others how to benefit from learning the art of social media. Maybe you are passionate about a cause and want to make the world a better place. Just doing a Google search on a topic that interests you will open up a vast array of choices. The internet is teeming with more information than anyone could ever begin to absorb. So pick a topic that blows your hair back and begin.

Pick Your Topic

There are numerous needs you can meet by the topics you choose, and there are hundreds of topics to choose from. Everything from detective who-done-it stories to vampires and werewolves. You may be a dog groomer and could write on how to groom dogs, or how to get your kids to love vegetables, or the correct way to do Yoga. There should be something that gets you excited enough to sit down and write. My sister Carol is an interior designer, but now that she is retired, she restores old unique pieces of furniture. Her home is like a museum, and every time I visit, there is always something special she has created. She could write a great book on how to strip and refinish antiques, complete with her own pictures. You could write your own book about retiring and having a blast rebuilding old motors or antique cars. Remember, you are writing to meet a need.

The art of grand parenting could be an interesting topic, or tips for parenting teens. You may want to write a book dedicated to your children and their life growing up. You could tell some interesting stories about each child and the intricate relationships of siblings. Children always love to hear stories, especially about them.

Tell Your Secrets

Colorful ancestors might be a challenge, especially if they are still alive! This is where the art of disguise comes into the picture. If Uncle Wilson was having an affair with the next door neighbor's wife, and Aunt Ethel shot both of them, you may want to embellish the story, and by changing names and descriptions it will keep you out of hot water with relatives. Historical fiction could be based on truth but with disguised characters. Remember, the beauty of storytelling is what sells books, and in books we can say anything we want, as long as we are not slandering someone. So be careful when you tell stories about people you know, unless they are good stories, and you either have their permission, or if necessary, you change their names and physical description.

One of the most popular subjects for self-publishing is writing your family genealogy. The main motive is to present family with copies of your research in the form of a book, with your name on the cover, of course! It is so wonderful to have family history preserved in a book. It seems extra special when it is in a published book. You could even do a new twist on a genealogy book by adding colorful stories and photos of ancestors that were handed down through the generations. There might even be enough juicy information you uncover to write a novel. While my daughter Alison was researching our family history, she discovered that a great-great uncle died of moonshine poisoning!

People Need Your Stories

There are a myriad of topics to choose from, but the most important part is to write about something you enjoy. I personally love to write non-fiction, especially self-help inspirational books, and I am an avid reader of them. I research my topics by reading other author's works. I get many ideas from the books I read. Do I copy them, no! That is called plagiarism. Do I steal ideas from them, yes! Any time you are using ideas from another author, give that author credit. If you are using quotes from their work, this is acceptable, as long as you are not quoting the whole book! Be certain you state their name and the book you quoted from.

You might have great stories about retirement and having a blast. Maybe you own a bed and breakfast and could share how you chose the location and purchased just the right home. Perhaps you converted your own home into a bed and breakfast. What problems did you incur and what legal hurdles did you have to jump through? Share your first opening day and how it went. Are you running your new business as a couple or are you on your own? Tell about the cooking experiences and catching the kitchen on fire. In one of my stays at a bed and breakfast in Scotland, the gentleman of the house shared how upset he was that his wife wanted to convert

What Should I Write About?

their beautiful estate into a bed and breakfast. He finally gave in, but made it very clear that he was never going to help or be involved in any way. Our host was literally a retired rocket scientist, and was telling me this story while he was pouring my morning coffee and serving my breakfast. It sure would make an amazing book like the best seller, *A Year in Provence*.

Oh My Heart

I recently met an interesting young woman who writes Romance books. She sells 5,000 books per month! I am not talking about erotica type romance. I am talking about "soft romance." Think Sleepless in Seattle with Tom Hanks and Meg Ryan. This is the type of story romance books are made of. A friend once gave me a book titled "Love in the Afternoon." It was definitely not my type of read, but guess what? They made a movie from that book! It was only about 175 pages. Amazing! Perhaps you could entertain us with your own love story. Hmmm.

Tell Us How

Are you a great organizer? Is your home so well-organized that there is not one thing out of place and not a speck of dust anywhere? Everybody wants to *get organized*. Well, maybe you can tell them how. Describe how you go about your day and the process of being orderly. How did you learn to be so organized; was your mother organized? Maybe neatness is an obsession and you spend every minute at being orderly. How has this habit affected your life and that of other family members? It may be fun for you to clean, dust, and sort, so tell us how we can do it too!

Do you love pets? What do you love about pets and what type of pet do you have? My friend Bill has a pet parrot and it has never been around another parrot, yet it routinely makes a nest under his kitchen sink and lays eggs. His bird called Rocky got her name because any time Bill has friends over for a visit, his parrot rocks back and forth until they leave. Rocky is very jealous and has to be caged whenever company visits, as he has bitten two guests and cannot be trusted. Rocky not only sits on Bill's shoulder to watch television but also goes to the pool and sits on the back of the lounge chair to ward off unwelcome guests. I think this could be a great story for parrot lovers, especially the part when Rocky was sitting on Bill's shoulder and laid two eggs that slid inside the front of his shirt. There is something wrong with this picture Bill!

People Need Your Advice

Self-help books are a great choice as people are always looking for advice and help with their various issues. There is something gratifying when we can give direction or encouragement to others in need. Giving guidance and improving lives is incredibly rewarding and self-help books allow you to connect with your reader on a deeper level. My first self-help book tells my own personal journey through divorce and how I struggled to regain my equilibrium and find balance in my life mentally, physically, social-emotionally, and spiritually. I had to come to grips with the fact that my life as I had known it was now over. Learning to cope with what life had dealt me was a real challenge. I learned that my husband had left me for a woman I had known for several years and she was twenty years younger! Releasing my anger and resentment was a long process, but carrying the bitterness was too great a price. My story was written to help other women who have suffered the loss of their marriage and lifestyle through divorce. Many women have contacted me to thank me for writing "*You Lost Your Marriage Not Your Life*" just for them. Maybe you should consider writing your own personal story.

A friend paid me a visit when I was at my lowest after my divorce, and what did she hand me? A book of course! She gave me Joan River's book, "Bouncing Back." Joan tells her personal story of loss, with the suicide of her husband, her Broadway play closing, and the bankruptcy of her jewelry business. Whatever your opinion of Joan Rivers, her book helped encourage me so much. That was years ago, and I still have that book. Remember what I said about people not wanting to part with their books!

Answer Their Questions

People buy self-help books because they want to change some problem or issue in their life. Maybe you have a story about a serious health issue you have overcome and you could help others. Your book may just hold the answer they have been searching for. The information must have meaning or value for the reader. If you have to research your topic, it must be accurate. People are internet savvy and will not appreciate false information. Does your book answer the questions you present? The reader does not want a documentary, they want a story, your story!

Define Your Niche

Let's look at the term *defining your niche*. Although it is nice to fantasize about selling your book to the entire world, that is exactly what it is—a fantasy. You must decide who your book is written for, and trust me on this one, it is not written for everybody. Your niche is defined by your specialty, which is specific to your interest, ability, or nature. How can you stand out from your competition? Answering this question will play a major role in keeping you focused. For instance, if your topic is children's books, you must begin to narrow your niche.

What age will you target for your books and how will you reach your target? Maybe you want to write a book that you will market to schools regarding the food

What Should I Write About?

served in the cafeteria. With thousands of schools throughout the country, it would be difficult to visit all of them. This is where maybe a spinoff product, like a CD, could work well for you. You could also create a brochure to advertise your book and send it to schools. We will discuss more spinoff ideas in a later chapter.

"Stories are living and dynamic. Stories exist to be exchanged. They are the currency of Human Growth."—Jean Houston

What really blows your hair back?

_____
_____
_____
_____
_____
_____
_____
_____

What topic do you know that really gets you excited?

_____
_____
_____
_____
_____
_____
_____
_____

What Should I Write About?

Can you think of a new twist to put on an old subject?

_____

_____

_____

_____

_____

_____

_____

_____

Do you love to tell stories?

_____

_____

_____

_____

_____

_____

_____

What interesting scenarios could you come up with to flush out stories?

_____
_____
_____
_____
_____
_____
_____
_____
_____

What niche would you like your book to target?

_____
_____
_____
_____
_____
_____
_____
_____
_____

Chapter 3
RESEARCH RESEARCH RESEARCH

The greatest part of a writer's time is spent in reading. In order to write, a man will turn over half a library to make one book."
—Samuel Johnson

Tell It Your Way

Okay, we have reviewed various ideas and once you pick your own topic and genre, you are ready to begin your research. Read, read, and read. Research your subject on Amazon and see if there are others who have written a similar book as you plan to write. If you do not find even one book on your subject, it may be a good reason to pick a new topic. There might not be too many people who want to learn how to raise camels in Alaska. On the other hand, if you see popular books on your subject, that means people are interested, and chances are if you write a great book, they will purchase yours as well. I have learned so much by reading other writer's work on my topic or niche. This provides valuable information that you can use for your book. Once again, remember that we do not copy other writer's work, we simply glean information and put it in our own words. If you are using a quote from a book you have researched, be certain to put it in quotes, followed by that author's name.

Read Other Author's Work

My library is full of books by other authors that I purchased for ideas for my books and I really do not want to part with any of them. They are like my babies and what if I need them for reference? Even though I do have a Kindle, I still love to hold a book in my hands, and I hate to mark them up. It seems like a crime to red line and dog ear my books. However, you have my permission to dog ear and mark up this book any way you like. Okay, back to writing your book. Now that you have your topic, where do you begin? Great writers read other authors work. In other words, it is imperative that you read and keep abreast of what books are out there in your genre. Reading is also extremely valuable in honing your writing skills. Read other stories similar to what you wish to write about and see how your brain starts to organize thoughts and ideas into possible story lines. What do other authors have to say about your topic and how could you put a new spin on an old subject?

Research Research Research

"Read, read, read. Read everything—trash, classics, good and bad, and see how they do it. Just like a carpenter who works as an apprentice and studies the master. Read!"
—William Faulkner

Start at the Beginning
The most important thing is to know your material and if not, then re-examine your motive for writing about it. If you have a subject you are passionate about, but know little on the subject, you must learn it. We are blessed not only with amazing libraries but also with the internet at our fingertips. Remember college term papers and countless hours spent at the local library reading and researching? Well, now we have choices. I highly recommend that new authors read other authors work as I mentioned earlier, because it will help you create your own style and voice.

Google Your Topic
The more you know about your chosen topic, the better. Today's readers are savvy about information presented to them. They quickly decide if the author is authentic and knowledgeable of their subject. With a few clicks of their mouse and a Google search, they can verify anything. If you want to master your subject, you must research and read.

Doing a Google search on your topic is also a means to gleaning information and ideas for your book. There are numerous articles and videos on Google and you can easily get lost in a sea of data. So stick to your intended subject and stay on target to research your book idea. You should be able to flush out some great tidbits from your research. You will also see other authors promoting their books on Google, as well as their websites and press releases. Just snoop around and check these out, as it never hurts to see what your competition is up to.

How Are Others Doing It
While you are busy conducting your research, notice how other authors are promoting their books. Many are giving away free seminars and webinars as a means to sell more books. If you love to talk, love to teach, and love to meet new people, you will see hundreds of ways to get the word out about your book. More on promoting later.

Look Inside
Amazon has made it easy to peruse books we are interested in without having to purchase them. You can even buy used books for as little as one cent. The *Look Inside* feature is a great resource for reviewing chapter headings and descriptions. You can even review the pitch on the back cover copy and see what others in your

genre and niche have to say. If you like what they say, and it applies to your book, put it in your own words and make it better. The important thing is that as you write, you find your own style and method of storytelling. Even a three or four hundred page novel is merely a bunch of stories woven together to create colorful characters, mystery, and intrigue.

Know When to Move Forward

Know when enough research has been done and get on with the project of writing your book. I did so much research on my first book and ended up with mountains of papers that at times it completely overwhelmed me. Thanks to Dan Poynter and his book "The Self-Publishing Manual," I was able to organize my mess. Dan says to purchase a large three ring binder with a zipper and insert pages with a pocket on each side. Label each page tab with your chapter titles and sort your research pages and place them in the correct order of your chapters. This is a good way to organize your material and eliminate what you don't need or save it for your next book. I wound up with a super thick binder, but what I loved about the zipper was I could keep all my paper safe.

Keep It Together

I started using file folders as a young woman when I was selling real estate. I could never find anything and my boss walked into my office one day and said, "Barbara, I want to teach you an easy way to sort out this mess." I was so embarrassed but happy to hear it was an *easy way*. He handed me a box of file folders and said "Here, label these and file them alphabetically. When I come back in this office, I would really love to see the top of your desk!" Pretty simple advice and guess what, I still use file folders to stay organized, even if it only holds a sticky note. This will keep you from being overwhelmed!

"The best way to become acquainted with a subject is to write about it"
—Benjamin Disraeli

Research Research Research

Have you purchased or read books related to your topic?

____

Do you understand the value in reading others author's work?

What is it about your chosen topic that excites you?

_____
_____
_____
_____
_____
_____
_____
_____

Are you a good story teller?

_____
_____
_____
_____
_____
_____
_____
_____

Research Research Research

Do you have a plan for organizing your material?

Who will you write your book for?

Chapter 4
CHOOSING A PUBLISHER

"Every secret of a writer's soul, every experience of his life, every quality of his mind, is written large in his works."—Virginia Woolf

What Are Your Choices
How are you going to publish your book? There are only three choices and they are vanity publishing, self-publishing, or traditional publishing. Print on demand is often called Vanity or Indie Publishing. This is where you pay a publishing company or vanity press to handle all aspects of completing your book. Two popular ones are Lulu and Outskirts Press, but there are dozens more to choose from. Self-publishing means that you handle all aspects of bringing your book to print. You must set up a publishing company or if you already have a business, you can publish under your business name. You would also have to purchase your own International Standard Book Number or ISBN number from Bowkers. This special number identifies your book and its publisher. You will also have to purchase paper, do page layout, and hire a cover designer. In its truest form, you handle every detail of publishing, printing, selling, and shipping your books.

Keep Ownership of Your Book
Book sales are tracked by their ISBN numbers, so you will not want to skip this important step, unless it is your own family genealogy book, or eBook giveaways, and you do not intend to sell it. You still might want to add an ISBN to your genealogy book, just in case you decide to do lectures and teach others how to write their own family history book. They might like to purchase yours as a guide. Create Space will provide a free ISBN and include the book's price and a barcode, so in case you have opportunities to sell your book, you are prepared. However, when you accept a free ISBN through Create Space, and you decide to take your book elsewhere, you will need to purchase your own ISBN.

Just because you published with Create Space, it does not affect the ownership you have in your book. You still own it and it is 100% yours. However, if you decide to establish a company and publish under that name, you may want to have your own ISBN. Be prepared for sticker shock if you purchase a single ISBN. The going rate is $125.00 each. If you intend to publish a series of books, then it makes sense to purchase multiple numbers and receive a discount. This is why many self-published writers choose to accept a free ISBN from Create Space.

You will need a separate ISBN for your paperback version and hard cover versions. Remember, this is your tracking number for book sales, and you certainly want to receive the proper royalties for each type of book sold. Paperback books generally are a higher price tag than eBooks. For an eBook format, Amazon requires you to include an ASIN that is unique to eBook sales. Each book is different and each has a different price and its own unique number.

Which Way to Publish
If you decide to pursue traditional publishing, find an agent, and go that route, you will probably be looking at two long years before you ever see your book in print. This is, of course, after you have found an agent, and your agent has found a publisher willing to publish your book. You will also have to prepare a book proposal. Some authors have shared with me that it took as long to write the proposal as the book! Publishing houses get thousands of manuscripts that are stacked in the slush pile and are never even opened, let alone read. Most get dumped in the trash by overworked employees who just get tired of looking at the stacks of manuscripts taking up valuable space in their office.

There are only a handful of traditional publishing houses left and their primary focus is fame. If you are a star with a large media following, you are what they are looking for. Occasionally, a rogue first time author sneaks in with a great book and gets a contract, but they are few and far between. If I sound negative about traditional publishing houses, *I am*. Authors have been so discouraged by the insensitivity of agents and publishing houses that they totally abandon their writing. Don't let this be you! If you plan to seek an agent, there is a resource called *Writer's Market*. The book is a large manual with lists of agents and the particular genre's they specialize in. The book is very expensive and you can find it at most libraries or on the internet at: www.writersmarket.com.

It's Up to You
Many people have shared with me how they are working on a book. However, they want to go the traditional route and find a publisher, as they do not have the time to promote the book on their own and want the publisher to handle it for them. Sorry to be the bearer of bad news, but you are going to have a very rude awakening, because traditional publishing houses do not do anything more for you than you can do for yourself. The only difference is they issue an advance against royalties and maybe get your book in some bookstores. The odds of them making a

profit on an unknown author are very slim and most of the time, they do not even recoup the investment. They look to the author to have a marketing plan in place and to have a social media platform.

People love how-to non-fiction books that help them solve their problems, such as: self-improvement, health and wellness, how to earn a ton of money, love and sex, and mental and spiritual wholeness. These all make great books. If you are writing fiction, and can create a series, you will want your audience or fans to be anxiously waiting for your next book. Keep them informed by using social media and posting to your blog. Facebook fan pages, Twitter, and LinkedIn accounts are all great for this. Pinterest is also a great social media resource for promoting your books and pinning meaningful articles. We will discuss social media in another chapter.

You Need a Plan
In order to be really successful as an author, you need a plan. You cannot go blindly into the night and find your way, and the same is true with writing and publishing your book. That being said, let's consider choosing your publisher. I like to have this established in the beginning stages of your book, because this allows you to follow a format for that particular publisher. I have chosen to recommend Amazon's company, called Create Space, for print books and their digital company, Kindle Direct Publishing or KDP, for eBook's. I recommend these two Amazon companies as they provide the fastest, easiest, and least expensive way to publish your book.

Peruse Other Books
You should visit Amazon and review other books in your genre so you have an idea of the cover and layout you want for your book. If your book will be about cooking, gardening, or organizing, you may want to use pictures. How many pictures you will need, and if you intend to use color, makes a difference. Children's books will definitely need colorful pictures and unique sizes. There are a myriad of ways to design your book. Once you have an idea of what you want your book to look like, keep that image in mind as you begin writing your book.

Your Title is Your Headline
Some of you may remember the news boys who used to stand on corners and yell, "Extra, extra, read all about it!" That was how they sold newspapers in the cities. Choose your working title, *your headline*, as this will help keep you focused. It does not have to be your final title. Don't be married to your original title. I had chosen a title for my first book and when I researched on Amazon, there were at least a dozen

same or similar titles. I decided to choose a different title. You may want to change your title if a more suitable title comes to mind in your writing process.

Even though you may have a general idea as to the type of cover you want and have chosen a designer, do not actually create your cover yet. You may decide to change the title and it might require a different cover design than you originally thought. Think of your title as a headline in a newspaper. Would you buy your book based on the title you chose? The cover may draw people in, but the key to getting them to open your book is *the title*. "How To" are still the leading two words to showcase your headline, like the "Buy Now" button on most retail websites.

Share the Benefit

Potential buyers for your book need to see the benefit in purchasing your book. "How to" makes a promise and addresses the WIIFM that they are looking for and anticipating. Research your title on Amazon to see if someone has that exact title. You cannot copy write your title, and there are several of the same titles. However, if you decide to call your book Harry Potter, you would have a problem because Harry Potter is also a trademark, just like the Chicken Soup for the Soul books. You really do not want to publish a title that has already been over used. Get creative and create your own!

Is It Catchy?

Try to choose a catchy title and keep it to no more than 5 words. Most books also have a sub-title, which generally gives a little more detail regarding what your book is about. You can use the sub-title to add key words, but be careful not to add too many keywords, as this is called stuffing and Amazon frowns on that tactic. There is a book publisher called Lulu and they have a nice feature on their website, which you can visit at www.lulu.com/titlescorer/index.php. Follow their simple instructions and they will rate your book title. There is no charge for this and it is really fun to see where your title rates. By rate, I mean give you the percentage range of the chances your title could become a bestseller.

Your title is critical to whether your book sells or not. Unless you already have a following and they are anxiously waiting for your next book, you must carefully select a dynamic title. Do not get so hung-up on the title that you put off writing your book. Just pick the best working title and sub-title you can come up with and begin.

"I love writing. I love the swirl and swing of words as they tangle with human emotions.
—James Michener

How will you publish your book?

___

How much of the publishing aspects do you want to handle personally?

___

Choosing a Publisher

Have you researched titles and topics on Amazon to see what your competition is writing?
___

___

___

___

___

___

___

___

Have you chosen a working title for your book?
___

___

___

___

___

___

___

___

Can you list some benefits you want your readers to experience?

Can you narrow down your topic to a specific niche?

Chapter 5
START AT THE BEGINNING

"The research is the easiest. The outline is the most fun. The first draft is the hardest, because every word of the outline has to be flushed out. The rewrite is very satisfying."
—Ken Follette

Yes, You Need an Outline

Just like they taught us in school, start at the beginning—with an outline. I cannot stress this enough because as the old saying goes, *if you don't know where you are going, any road will take you there*. If you fail to outline, you fail to have a road map to follow, and you may end up at a dead end or going off a cliff! Think of your outline as your GPS to keep you on the right track and help prevent you from getting lost. You will be meandering all over the map without an outline. Even a book on genealogy must be outlined and laid out properly, or Uncle Joe may look like he was born after his children.

Order Please

When outlining your book, every detail must be in order, well thought out, and researched, especially if you are giving a lot of facts. Even though you start at the beginning, always keep the end in sight to keep your focus. First, purchase a three ring old fashion binder and a pack of lined paper with pre-punched holes. Don't worry, I have a reason for this. When you do your outline the way you did it in school, you will be able to move the pages and chapters around if they fit better elsewhere. Maybe you realize that chapter four should actually be chapter six. Since you are going to start your outline with chapter titles, you can easily play around with the organizing without too much trouble. You can do the same thing on your computer and just copy and paste anything you want to move or insert into a different chapter. Your outline will help you determine how many chapters you need for your book. You will want to have at least ten or twelve chapters. If you are writing a novel, you will have several chapters, depending on the length of your book. With a well-planned, carefully structured outline for your book, you can avoid the common *writer's block* that so many authors complain about. You will also be way ahead of the game by finishing your book in record time.

Start at the Beginning

Get Organized

I am a firm believer in organizing your material before you begin to write. Several years ago, I owned a day spa. It was in a mall and required that I build out the interior to my own specifications. I went to a local beauty supply house to order the equipment. They advertised that they would lay out a design for you at no extra cost based on your measurements of the empty shell. I thought it sounded like a great plan. Oh boy. My builder took one look at the drawings and said, "Barbara, there is no way you will ever fit all of this equipment in this space. For one thing, when a person is sitting in the first shampoo chair, no one will be able to get past them to the other two chairs. Your massage table will fit in the room, but your massage therapist will not be able to walk around it without adding two more feet." I was mortified and had to have a whole new layout plan drawn up. I had definitely put the cart before the horse. No one mentioned that I would lose a foot on all sides when the walls were in place. I tell you this story to emphasize the value in an outline or a system to keep you on target.

What's Your Style

I realize there are those who cringe at the very thought of a formal outline. This primarily relates to my novel writers. I even have a friend who just sits down and begins writing. She tells me that she develops characters and then her books write themselves. She has an idea of where she wants the story to go and then just writes. There are many famous authors who have the same approach for writing their books. Stephen King states in his book *On Writing* that he always writes at least 10 pages a day, seven days a week. On the other hand, James Joyce, who is considered one of the greatest writers of the last century, took his time and labored over each individual sentence until it read to his liking. Truman Capote, author of *Breakfast at Tiffany's*, used to write with a pencil while horizontal. Yes, while lying down. Even though I personally get a lot of ideas and inspiration while lying down, I still have to sit up to write. Most writers state, however, that they prefer to write in the morning, when their mind is fresh. There is no right or wrong way to write your book, just be authentic, develop your own style, and *tell your stories*!

For those wishing to have more structure in preparing to write your book, using an outline is still a great choice. My main goal in writing this book was to help newbie writers create a cohesive manuscript. Researching and outlining your book will provide ease and speed to get the job done. You want your reader to get exactly what it is you are trying to say, so do not make them guess. Worse yet, you do not want them to shake their heads and say "What?" Make it easy for them to follow a sequence or, as I said earlier, make it read like a GPS.

An Organized Book Makes a Happy Reader

Once you have completed your research, follow this simple orderly way to organize your outline. First, open up Microsoft Word on your computer or open your three ring binder. Think about possible titles for each chapter. Use the most descriptive titles you can think of, as these will be the main support for your outline. Each chapter will have a separate page. You may want to shorten the chapter titles later. Label your chapters, starting with Chapter One, and continue. Next, think about how you outlined in school, and type the letter A under the chapter title and create a Sub-Chapter title. Below the sub-chapter title, write Paragraph One. Just provide a clear sentence, describing what paragraph one will say or do. Define the benefit in each chapter, always keeping in mind how it relates to your book's title and chapter description.

This information can even be used in the front of your book, where you list chapter titles and describe what is in each chapter. You may want to develop your outline in more detail. Now move to Paragraph Two and continue to do the same for at least ten or twelve paragraphs. Write something for each paragraph, even if it is just one or two sentences. From each paragraph, you will be able to develop additional paragraphs, but initially just keep it simple. Next, start a new page for Chapter Two and repeat the same outline. Once you start filling in the blanks, you will see your book take on a life of its own.

Make It Clear

In my book "Dancing in Rhythm with the Universe," I added a sub-title, 10 Steps to Choreographing Your Best Life. My title is a little obscure, and a sub-title was necessary for clarity, as I did not want potential readers to think my book was about actual dancing. The chapter titles are the basis of my outline, as each chapter is a life dance. The first chapter is titled Dance of Courage. After reading the back cover copy and having piqued their interest, the potential reader or buyer will probably look inside the book at the chapter titles to determine if anything fits the "What's in it for me?" that we talked about earlier. They will make a determination if the book is worthy of their time and investment. Some books have lengthy chapter descriptions, which read almost like an outline. There is no right or wrong way, just whatever works for you. Some chapter titles are questions that draw the reader in and arouse their curiosity. It is up to you to help convince them through your words that this book can solve their problem or entertain them.

Entertain Me

If your book is a novel, you will have to prove through your chapter descriptions and back of book copy that your book will entertain them from beginning to

Start at the Beginning

end, whether instructional, historical, amusing, mystery, sexy, or terrifying. This is your sales pitch opportunity, so make it good! Great sales copy sells books. Develop your outline as thoroughly as possible, because it will serve as the structure or foundation for your book. The reader expects you to take them on a journey, whether it's a thrilling trip or challenging, whatever your topic, they want to become part of the trip. They do not want to watch from the sidelines, they want to go on the trip with you! It is up to you to make that happen.

"Reading is the sole means by which we slip, involuntarily, often helplessly, into another's skin, another's voice, another's soul."
—Joyce Carol Oates

Do you understand the value in creating an outline?

Can you come up with 10 chapter titles?

Start at the Beginning

Have you researched or brainstormed to develop your one or two sentence paragraphs?

_____
_____
_____
_____
_____
_____
_____
_____

Can you begin to see how each step works off the other?

_____
_____
_____
_____
_____
_____
_____
_____

Do you now see the value of structuring each chapter?

_____
_____
_____
_____
_____
_____
_____

Are you focused on the finished product?

_____
_____
_____
_____
_____
_____
_____

Chapter 6
LET'S ROUGH IT

"You do not have to explain every single drop of water in a rain barrel. You have to explain one drop—H2O. The reader will get it."
—George Singleton

Write Like You Speak

Now it is time for your rough draft. A rough draft is exactly what it says, so don't try to write perfectly and attempt to edit your book as you write. If you keep going back and attempting to edit each paragraph, you will lose your momentum. Just use your outline and start writing. Write the way you speak to others, not some bunch of jargon. You do not want to sound like a college term paper, just be natural and let your words flow as if spoken. Keep your sentences tight, short, and concise, with no unnecessary words. Above all, do not ramble on and become too descriptive. Use only enough words to make it clear, all others are a waste. Give your reader the benefit of a doubt. Trust me, if it is written with as few words as possible and to the point, they will get it!

If your subject is too broad, you may need to narrow it down or write a series. The important thing is that you stay on target and remain true to your topic. Think about how you feel when reading another writer's work. If you do not like their work, ask yourself why? Then make sure you make it easy for your readers to follow a well-crafted, organized manuscript to a stupendous conclusion!

Create a Schedule

I like to write early in the morning, when my mind is fresh, but you might do better in the evening, when everyone else is in bed. I sometimes head to the beach to write, as I live in sunny Florida. Much of my inspiration comes to me at the beach. The important thing is that you create a schedule. Set a time each day to get alone with your book and write a minimum of three to four pages a day. This will give you 100 pages in thirty days. If you want your book to be longer, just simply write five or six pages a day. Remember, these are unedited pages, written as quickly as possible. Try not to labor over what you are going to say, just let the words free-flow onto the paper. Find a quiet spot where you will not be interrupted.

Let's Rough It

Give yourself permission to write anything that pops into your head. Later, when you go back and read what you wrote, you may say "WOW, did I write that? That is really good!" Make a regular date with yourself and your writing. It is vital that you do not work against your internal clock. Determine what works best for you and your writing schedule. If you do not have the luxury of a private office, then find a special place where you can write without distraction. One of my clients shared that he wrote much of his manuscript in his car! It was the only place he could go where he was not constantly interrupted by family members. Hey, whatever works.

If you have research yet to do, try writing at your local library, with thousands of books at your disposal. I have a friend who wrote two novels while having breakfast at a Hilton Restaurant. I always knew where she would be from 8 a.m. until 10 a.m. most week days. She shared with me how she could write several pages during that two hour time and was able to complete her books in less than a year. You could write a novel in one year by only writing a page a day. Remember, that year will go by anyway, so you might as well have it end with a finished book!

Keep Your Focus

Perseverance is the key, so keep your eye on the target and your fingers on the keyboard. If you get stuck, then step away from it and take a breather. There is no point in having a melt-down over writing a book. Each day will propel you forward to write and finish your book. Think of it this way: publishing your book makes you *immortal*! Now that is a concept to give pause. Your book will live on long after you have departed, so get to it and write. Don't stop and try to analyze your writing, as this will undermine your creativity. Just keep writing, as there is plenty of time to edit when your rough draft is complete. There will always be distractions and interruptions in our plans and schedules, but return to your objective as quickly as possible, which is to write your book!

I used to write my books in cursive, but now I do most of my writing on my computer, as it saves a lot of time. Type your work in Microsoft Word, as this is what most publishers want. Some, however, will only accept your book in a PDF file. There are several programs that will convert your file to a PDF version. Make certain that you are using spell check and that you save your work several times while you are typing on your computer, just in case you should have a power outage. Nothing is more depressing than losing your work and then having to try and recreate what you lost.

I always have my husband, David, read my rough draft, as I totally trust him to give an honest opinion. However, be careful who you share your manuscript with and don't email it to anyone who might pass it on to others. People are sometimes too eager to pass an opinion and they might just be a little jealous and attempt to derail you. Don't let the dream robbers hold you up and steal your dreams. Just focus on your goal, which is holding your finished book in your hands!

Putting It All Together

There are several components or parts that need to be incorporated into your book. If you have a connection to anyone with name recognition to write a foreword for your book, that is amazing. However, if not, no problem, as many books do not have a foreword. We already mentioned the copyright page, which follows the inside title page. Next will be your dedication. You do not need to have a dedication page, but I highly recommend it. What special person or persons were valuable to you as you went about the task of writing your book? These are usually family members or best friends. Recognizing them is a wonderful gesture, and they will love seeing their name in a book.

Give a Nod

Next is your acknowledgements page, providing you have someone or something to praise. This might be people you know who have helped prepare your manuscript or proof read it for you. Maybe someone was a professional photographer and took pictures for you. Just peruse other author's books for ideas. Next will be your contents page, listing each chapter. This is where your outline will be valuable. Some authors elect to write long descriptive sentences detailing what each chapter contains; just don't end up writing the whole chapter. This is extremely valuable in letting potential buyers learn more of what they will find inside your book. Next would be your introduction page, which is generally written by the author, describing what the book is about. Once again, if someone is contemplating purchasing your book, why not help them with a description of what they can expect to learn from your book.

Shine

Now you can take advantage of your opportunity to shine. At the end of your book is a perfect place to list further information about you! If you plan to sell your books on your website, you must tell your reader how to find it. Also, this is the place to list your web address, blog address, and of course, your email! Do not skip this free marketing opportunity to list your social media addresses and let people know how to contact or connect with you. About the Author generally comes at the back of the book, although some authors place it in the front of the book. Either way is acceptable. List any credentials you may have or lectures you have given that relate to your book topic. You will not want to miss out on any speaking gigs that might come your way.

Let's Rough It

Following will be a page titled Cited Works or Bibliography. This is where you list by chapters the title of each book, article, or resource you cited, quoted, or referenced throughout your book. Give other authors credit for their works. If you did a lot of research, you may want to include a Suggested Reading list of books from your research related to your subject. These added features will make your book look professional and complete.

Give a Benefit

The back of your book is also where to list any promotional material, such as an offering of something beneficial to the reader, like an eBook or a special report. Your bonus is a tool to get the reader to visit your website. This is your chance to capture emails. To do this, you will have an opt-in box or a capture page for visitors to sign-in to get your gift. There are several people on Fiverr to create your opt-in box or capture page for you. The gift must be perceived as valuable by your guest or they will hit the delete key and move on. The bonus gift can be anything of interest that relates to your writing. For instance, if you have written a book on Health and Fitness, you might want to offer a free eBook with your favorite recipes. If your book is about antique cars, you might give a special report on where antique car collectors gather.

Choose Your Editor

Okay, now that you have written your book, the next step is editing. It is very difficult to edit your own work, unless you are an English major. It is easy to pass over misspelled words or misused words when you are editing your own work. One method to use if you are self-editing is to enlarge your typed manuscript to 150%. You will be amazed at how the errors will stand out. You want your book to be as error free as possible. After you have gone over your manuscript thoroughly, take a break and then start from the end and work backward. Most mistakes are generally in the last half of the book and missed by tired eyes.

I used First Editing to edit my book "Dancing in Rhythm with the Universe: 10 Steps to Choreographing Your Best Life," and they did a great job and were very reasonably priced. I also used them for this book, as they sometimes make suggestions to rearrange paragraphs or chapters for a better flow. I am not affiliated with First Editing. They offer other publishing services as well. You can check them out at www.firstediting.com.

"To me, the greatest pleasure of writing is not what it's about, but the inner music that words make."—Truman Capote

Have you explored the possibilities for your book on Create Space?

_____
_____
_____
_____
_____
_____
_____
_____

Have you developed your working title and sub-title?

_____
_____
_____
_____
_____
_____
_____
_____

Let's Rough It

Have you created your chapter titles and sub-chapter titles?

Do you have a detailed outline of your book?

Have you detailed ten to twelve paragraphs per chapter?

What do you envision your finished book looking like?

Chapter 7
NOW LET'S PUBLISH YOUR BOOK

"People don't want more information. They want faith, in you, your goals, your success, in the stories you tell."—Annette Simmons

Create Space

The beauty of publishing through Create Space is that you can pick and choose how much of the publishing process you intend to do and how much you want to turn over to Create Space. You can use Create Space to self-publish or do a combination of self-publishing and Indie publishing. Even if you want to handle the whole process, Create Space will guide you in the steps. The first place to start is to have your book typed as a Word document. At this point in time, Create Space charges $349.00 to do the internal *basic* layout of your book.

The layout is critical, because you want the pages and chapters to end up in the right places on the pages of your book. For instance, you do not want Chapter Two to end up at the bottom of the last page of Chapter One. However, if you want to do it yourself and your document meets Create Space's specifications, by all means go for it. You might even be able to get your layout done cheaper through eLance or Fiverr. Be careful who you hire, as you want them to be familiar with Create Space and their specifications. Whichever source you choose, you want to be proud of your book and present it as a professional looking product that someone would like to buy and read.

Publish With Ease

Create Space has a system in place to help you publish your book with ease. In fact, they will not allow you to move ahead until you have met certain requirements. For instance, you must fill out every detail as you set-up your Create Space author account. Once you have met that criteria, you will be ready to upload your manuscript. Don't worry about uploading your book cover file yet, as Create Space only lets you go one step at a time. If there are any issues with your manuscript, they will email you within a day or two and instruct you to login to your Create Space account and fix any problems that may exist. Once you have done that, you will be able to move to the next step.

Now Let's Publish Your Book

If you are totally confused, they make it really easy to email or call them. They will even mail you a free copy of the interior of your book, minus the cover, so you can proof read for accuracy before it's published. You will get another proof once your cover has been approved. I highly recommend that you accept this service and carefully read your book before giving your final approval for printing. Get someone you trust to read your book, as they are not familiar with it and therefore may spot mistakes.

Create Space Has Your Back

It is no problem if you find mistakes after your book has been published, as you can simply upload a corrected version at any time. To correct any typos or errors you discover, you must login to your Amazon Create Space account to make the corrections. You will be directed to open the file and make the corrections and then upload this new version. The old version will automatically cancel out. I suggest that you review your book one more time, just to catch any missed typos, and you are good to go.

If you do happen to find mistakes in the first book Create Space sends you, simply login to your account and follow the directions to make necessary corrections. Yes, they will send you another book at no extra charge for your approval. To approve the final copy, you must log in to Create Space, go to your author page, and upload the interior book file. The next step will be your awesome cover. If you had it created by a professional cover designer, they will have put it in the proper file to meet Create Space's criteria. You will find the details for designing the book cover in Chapter 8.

Give It a Review

Create Space has added a new feature to help you publish your book. It is called Interior Reviewer. This program lets you see a virtual version of the interior file of your book. The beauty of using IR is you can easily spot any problem with the interior layout. Interior Reviewer will automatically highlight any issues that need to be corrected. This free tool accepts multiple file types, including, pdf, .doc, and .docx. The main reason you would use the Interior Reviewer is if you plan to do your own interior layout and want to see if there are any problems you need to fix.

Don't Miss Out

A word of caution about an opportunity you will not want to miss on Create Space. If you want your book to be eligible for libraries, you **must** purchase the LCCN, or Library of Congress Control Number, **before** you have approved your final proof. The fee for this service is $25.00. Once you have approved your proof, it is no longer available. Once you purchase the LCCN, Create Space will handle it all for you, but your book must have a Create Space ISBN. If you are a company using your own ISBN, you will not qualify for this service. This does not mean you can never have your book in libraries, it just means Create Space will not help you. You simply have to contact the libraries yourself.

Create Your Kindle eBook

Once you have your manuscript complete for Create Space, there is no good reason why you shouldn't create your Kindle eBook. You have already done the bulk of the work with your paperback book, so why lose out on profiting from an eBook? Kindle eBooks outsold paperbacks this past year on Amazon and you would perhaps be missing out on a money making opportunity. Digital books are not the wave of the future, the future is now! Kindle books can be read on Android and Apple devices.

If you choose to have Create Space lay out your eBook, the fee is $79.00. You can upload your eBook yourself at no charge. I had Create Space do my eBook layout as I wanted it to display properly on the Kindle reader. Of course, the amount of money you make with your book is directly related to a quality product and tenacious marketing. Amazon is constantly opening up opportunities around the world to market your books. Don't procrastinate another day to take advantage of the Amazon platform designed to help you sell your books! Amazon Kindle book sales total over 65% of all eBook sales. Do not miss this amazing opportunity to make your book a Kindle best seller.

If you plan to create an eBook from your manuscript, it requires a different layout. The major difference is that eBooks do not have page numbers. It is a continual flow on your Kindle or eBook reader, so you want to be certain that it meets Kindle Direct Publishing, or KDP, requirements. You will not be able to use bullets for your book interior, but you can use them on your book's cover. If you have KDP do your eBook layout, they will charge the $79.00 fee, however, you can do it yourself as we have discussed for free. They will take out any bullet points as well as page numbers. Amazon continues to make it easier for authors to see their books in print, so there is no reason to go elsewhere. You want your eBook to look as professional as possible, as it is a reflection on you as the author.

Don't Miss Out

According to the latest Amazon statistics, it is good business to publish both a paperback physical book and an Amazon Kindle eBook. There are still a huge

Now Let's Publish Your Book

number of people who do not own a Kindle and will only buy physical books. They are not remotely interested in anything digital. You do not want to miss this mature market and, with the low cost of publishing, there is no reason to compromise. Also, a thought to ponder, have you ever seen a book signing with an eBook?

"It's none of their business that you have to learn to write. Let them think you were born that way."—Ernest Hemingway

Have you decided how much of the publishing process you intend to do?

___

Do you have someone you trust to read your book?

___

Now Let's Publish Your Book

Do you intend to publish both a paperback and eBook?

_____
_____
_____
_____
_____
_____
_____
_____

Do you understand the difference between the paperback and eBook?

_____
_____
_____
_____
_____
_____
_____
_____

Chapter 8
CREATE A SHOW STOPPING COVER

"Inspiration is wonderful when it happens, but the writer must develop an approach for the rest of the time....The wait is simply too long."—Leonard S. Bernstein

Look Professional

There are so many options for creating a fabulous cover, and if you are not skilled in layout and design, leave it to the pros! Nothing will kill your sales more than an unprofessional looking cover. This is where you should invest most of your book's cost. If a cover doesn't show well, whether it is a print book or digital eBook, chances are a potential buyer will not purchase it. The width of the cover spine is critical, as in a perfect binding the cover is one continual sheet, so the spine must be accurate or your cover could be too big or too small. In other words, the spine might run over onto the front or back cover, which looks very unprofessional.

Create Space and KDP have several choices in helping you with cover design, and they will work with your own graphics as long as they meet their specifications. Create Space has design formats and styles to assist you if you wish to create your own cover. However, I did not use them for Dancing in Rhythm with the Universe, as I wanted to work directly with a professional cover designer. I found Karrie Ross on Dan Poynter's newsletter. Dan wrote "Self-Publishing Manual, How to Write, Print and Sell Your Own Book." This book is a must read if you intend to literally self-publish your own book from A to Z. Even if you do not intend to self-publish, there are great tips in this book.

Wow Your Reader

Now it is time to decide if you want to let Create Space or Kindle Direct Publishing design your cover, design it yourself, or hire a professional cover designer. The reason I want you to consider your layout and cover now is you will then know the upfront cost of your book. For my first book, "You Lost Your Marriage Not Your Life," I did not use a professional cover designer. I did it myself and it was not the best, but it was okay and kept the cost down. However, with my next book, I decided to use a professional cover designer, and it turned out awesome. I was even

Create a Show Stopping Cover

able to get my book on the shelf of Barnes and Noble in Naples, Florida. That is not easy to do for a self-published book, and I believe the cover played a major role in that accomplishment.

My recommendation is that you hire a professional cover designer, as this is a major factor in book sales. If you are a graphic designer or have experience in layout and design, then by all means design your own cover. It is all relevant to what you want to do with your book. A great resource for graphics for your cover is at www.istock.com. You can purchase photos or artwork from istock and you then own the right to use it. Whether you use a professional cover designer or opt to do it yourself, at least you will have a good idea of what you want. The designer I chose was Karrie Ross at www.karrieross.com. I am not affiliated in any way. Her minimum charge is $695.00 and up, depending on the size and number of images used. You should also explore eLance at: www.elance.com and www.fiverr.com, as they have several listings for cover designers. I used visualarts at Fiverr to design this cover. Book Baby, www.bookbaby.com, is another resource for your book.

Dynamic Trio
You have no doubt all heard the saying, "You can't judge a book by its cover." Well unfortunately, that is not true when applied to purchasing a book. Remember, you are competing with thousands of covers, like the flashing billboards of Times Square, all saying, "Buy me, buy me." Even though the **title** is number one for importance, the **cover** is equally as important, and then your **back cover information**. This makes up your extraordinary trio!

Make your cover a show stopper. This is the wrapping for your masterpiece, make it wonderful. It is representative of your work and reflects on you as an author. Most people spot your cover before ever zeroing in on the title. Experts tell us you have approximately four seconds to grab their attention on the front cover and 14 seconds on the back. If they like what they see so far, they will read the cover copy. The cover copy is your sales pitch and if the WIIFM doesn't measure up, its bye bye sale! The title, cover design, and sales pitch on the back of your book holds the greatest value in promoting book sales.

The front cover of your book will be the first thing a potential buyer sees, so make it good. It is imperative that your title is in large enough print to be legible in a postage stamp size on Amazon. This is another reason why fancy script writing is not always a good choice, unless you are writing romance novels or children's books. Look at other books on Amazon in your genre and analyze the ones that look the best. Can you read the title? Can you read the sub-title? Make yours stand out! Your book's front cover should have your title, sub-title, and a meaningful descriptive sentence, and of course your name. Remember everything is there to do one thing—sell your book!

Keep It Simple

The back cover must be clean and easy to read, with clearly outlined bullet points and without being too wordy. Do not and I say **do not** use numerous styles of print and several different colors for the back of your book! It is not a used car lot. If you are not good at writing sales copy, it should be another step left to the pros. If you plan to do it yourself, look at other books in your genre and see what they say. Don't copy theirs; just use different words to apply to your book. Write a short introduction at the top, three or four sentences at the most. This could be done in bold 14 pt. print to make it stand out. Your bullet points should follow. Keep them short and punchy to arouse interest. Use four to seven bullets.

You want to keep it a clean, quick, and easy read. Resist the urge to fill up the entire back cover with copy! Include your author blurb and a small thumbnail professional photo of you. Include your email and website address. Make it easy for people to contact you for radio, television, or speaking engagements. Even if you are not well known, you must establish your avatar and use this photo for all of your social media connections and advertising. Remember, people buy from those they know, like, and trust.

Stay Traditional

The spine of your book must be treated with the same importance as the rest of your cover. Think about seeing your book on the shelves of Barnes and Noble. It will be sandwiched between a myriad of other books on your subject, with only the spine showing for identification. In order for Create Space to print copy on a spine, your book must be at least 100 pages in length, so keep this in mind while writing your book. You can still have a spine if your book is under 100 pages, but minus any writing. The spine should contain only three things: your book's title, your name, and the publisher logo. Do not include your sub-title, as it will make the spine hard to read and look amateurish. Resist the urge to do anything too far from the norm as it will scream "Self-published!" As an example, one author puts his spine information vertical. Yes, it makes a statement, but not necessarily a positive one. Once you are famous, create your book cover any way you choose. For now, try and stay with the traditional style.

Choose Wisely

The binding you choose for your book will depend on the type of book you are writing. The standard choice is called *perfect binding* or a square spine. Perfect

Create a Show Stopping Cover

binding is used on the majority of paperback books. There are several different types of binding, depending on the style of book you wish to present. A cookbook or some children's books may require a *lay-flat binding*. The size you choose for your book is also important, especially if you are on a budget. The standard paperback is 5 ½ inches by 8 ½ inches. This size allows the printer to get more pages from a run, as the standard sheet of paper is 8 ½ inches by 11 inches. Your book can be printed more cheaply by sticking with this size, except of course, children's books and hard cover novels. Create Space does not offer hard cover for your books.

Blaze a Trail

Once you have your cover designed and ready, this is the time to create your book trailer. You will need the photos you used in your book cover to use in your Book Trailer. You also want to use the bullet points on the back cover for your trailer. Yes, you need one and before you cringe and start wondering how much this will cost you, remember the Fiverr gigs. Yes, you can have a professional book trailer done for five bucks! You can go to my YouTube Channel at: www.youtube.com/barbarasmil, then click my Channel in the upper left-hand side, and see all my promotional videos for my books. Each one cost me five bucks. Log in to Fiverr at www.fiverr.com and in the search box on the top right type in **petra7bat** and purchase one of her gigs for your book trailer. Petra will even provide legal music for your trailer. If you are uncertain as to which gig to buy, just send her a message by clicking the **contact the seller** and she will get back to you fairly soon.

Shop Around

Amazon's price for a trailer is outrageous and you can get a much better deal elsewhere. Their standard 30 second trailer is $1,199.00 and the premium 60 second trailer is $2,100.00. If you decide to do your own book trailer, you can still upload it to your author page on Amazon, provided it is first posted on You Tube. The reason Amazon and many other websites will only accept a video from YouTube is that they know that it is not a corrupt file. So do not attempt to upload a video directly from your website.

You gain strength, courage, and confidence by every experience in which you really stop to look fear in the face. You must do this thing you think you cannot do."—Eleanor Roosevelt

What decisions have you made about your cover?

___

___

___

___

___

___

___

___

Do you agree with the importance of a professional cover?

___

___

___

___

___

___

___

___

Create a Show Stopping Cover

Do you understand the value of your back cover copy?

___

What type of book are you writing and which binding works best?

___

Do plan to have you name and title on your book's spine?

_____
_____
_____
_____
_____
_____
_____

Do you see the value of a book trailer?

_____
_____
_____
_____
_____
_____
_____

Chapter 9
HOW TO PROMOTE YOUR BOOK

"The secret to getting started is breaking your complex overwhelming tasks into manageable tasks, and then starting on the first one."
—Mark Twain

Build a Platform

You might remember the movie about baseball where they said "Build it and they will come." Well, unfortunately that does not apply to "Write it and they will buy." Whether you publish your own book or get published through a traditional publishing house, no one is going to promote your book but you. Even major publishing houses look to the author and the platform they must provide to promote their books. How does one go about promoting their book? To start with, you need a website and your website needs a domain name or an address. A good place to register your domain name is Go-Daddy. They will even host your website for approximately $5.00 per month! They are very reasonable and I personally have several domains registered with Go-Daddy.

In choosing a domain name for your website, you want to use your book's title, or if you are lucky and have a following, you might want to use your own name. I use www.barbaraandcompany.com because I have had that domain since 1995, and it comes up on the front page of a Google search for any of my books or my name. If I would have known back then that I would write books full time, and that there was another Barbara Miller author, I would have secured other versions of my domain. Who knew?

Words of Wisdom

If you go with a vanity publisher, they will create an author website for you. However, a word of caution: if a vanity publisher creates a website for your book and you decide to take your book elsewhere, they will delete your author website. My first book, "You Lost Your Marriage Not Your Life," was initially published by a vanity press, and when I decided to go with Create Space, they deleted my author website and refused to give me the cover file for my book. They also kept my book up on Amazon and refused to remove it, saying it was up to Amazon to remove it. Amazon said they could not remove it either. So once you write and publish your book and put it on Amazon, it is there to stay.

If you are publishing through a vanity press, it is crucial that you totally understand the contract. Some vanity press companies will not release the files for your book! This means if you leave them, you will have to go through the process and expense of redoing the internal layout and design of your book. This also applies to the cover if they designed it for you. They will remove the ISBN they provided. Get everything in writing and review it carefully.

Give Your Book a Home
If you are self-publishing and are tech savvy, you can create your own author website with WordPress. For a nominal monthly fee, use Go-Daddy to host your website. Once you put your business up on WordPress, you own it and no one can decide to delete it but you. It is fairly simple, with a support team to help you, but an easier way is to hire Fiverr at: www.fiverr.com. Everything on Fiverr is five dollars. Their various services are referred to as gigs. When you choose a specific gig, they will produce the results in one to three days. They have numerous people who will create a website from WordPress for five bucks, as they say in Fiverr language. A friend of mine had Fiverr design her WordPress author website for $5.00 and it was up and running in 24 hours! Another great resource is eLance at: www.elance.com. They are a little more expensive than Fiverr, but still very reasonable.

Get Nosey
I suggest you check out some other author websites for ideas in how you would like yours to look. Remember, this is just for ideas, as you will want to make yours as original as possible. You should already have a professional photo of you from your book cover and that is exactly the same one you will use on your website. I know an author who dramatically changed her look after a few years and replaced her familiar avatar with a new picture. It took me a while before I even knew who she was. This is why you must have a professional photo taken, because you want people to recognize who you are. You will be posting this photo on all your social media sites, so make it good.

Show Off
A great photo of your book cover should also be added to your website, along with a well written About the Author blurb. This is all part of branding, and your

photo and book cover are your brand. Your author website is a great place to post photos of book signings, press releases, media copy, a book trailer, and anything that has to do with enhancing your brand. This is not a place for family photos or pictures of your pets, unless of course your book is about genealogy or pets.

PayPal to the Rescue

If you intend to sell your books on your website, you will have to incorporate a method of payment or shopping cart, and a Buy Now button, which will take the customer to a secure site to purchase your book or a button linking to Amazon. I personally use PayPal, but there are other companies to choose from, like E-Junkie. PayPal is known as the most secure shopping cart online and you do not want to lose a sale because a customer was afraid to process an order. Customers do not have to join PayPal in order to buy through PayPal, and they accept all major credit cards. Another feature PayPal offers is a small credit card processor that attaches right to your smart phone. However, you will need to set up an account with PayPal to get this free attachment. It is a wonderful tool to have when you are doing book signings.

Once you set up your PayPal account, you will be able to generate invoices for each sale to email to your customers. However, you may not want to process payments from your website, and that is okay because Amazon will do it all for you. People know, like, and trust Amazon, so who better to handle all of your book sales? The difference, however, is that when selling your books yourself, you get to keep most of the money instead of Amazon. If you intend to only publish an eBook and signup with Kindle Direct Publishing Select, you will not be able to sell it anywhere else. Just direct everyone to Amazon. I mentioned in an earlier chapter that when you publish on KDP Select, you agree to sell your eBook exclusively with KDP Select. Of course, this does not include your physical book, which you are free to market anywhere you choose.

The benefits of KDP Select is higher royalties and participation in KDP Select Global Fund. This is a fund Amazon created to encourage lending and borrowing of your eBook from Kindle Owner's Lending Library. Authors are paid a fee when their eBook is shared through the Lending Library.

Stay Connected

As an author, you will want to stay connected to your fans and customers. One way to do this is to capture their emails. This is something I cannot stress enough: it is imperative that you build your email list. In order to do this, you will need an opt-in or subscribe bar on your Author page. Potential customers will not opt-in unless you provide a good reason for them to do so. Offer them an incentive for sharing their email. This could be a sneak preview of your book, like a free chapter download, or an entertaining or informative article. Or, as we already discussed, include an offer in the back of your book that directs them to your website opt-in page. They must feel value in what you are offering, so think of something that might entice you to share your own email.

Blog about It

Okay, now you have your website and your masterpiece looking back at you every time you login to your website. What on Earth do you do next? It is very simple to add a blog to your new WordPress website or get someone to do it for you, like Fiverr or eLance. As a matter of fact, hire the same Fiverr tech to create your blog when they build your website. You will probably have to purchase two gigs, but for an additional 5 bucks, you will have a website and a blog. What a deal! Instruct your web designer or Fiverr tech to create a unique but similar look between your website and blog. You want your blog and website linked, or integrated, as this will rank your website higher in a Google search. Besides, if someone comes to your author website, you want them to stay and read your blog postings and opt-in for your newsletters. Post to your blog frequently, as this also helps you rank higher on Google

As you grow older, you'll find the only things you regret are the things you didn't do."
—Zachary Scott, Actor

Do you agree that you need a website?

Are you tech savvy enough to create your own blog?

Do you plan to sell on your website and see the need of a shopping cart?

Have you reviewed other author pages on Amazon's Author Central?

Have you checked out others opt-in boxes or a way to capture emails?

_____

_____

_____

_____

_____

_____

_____

_____

Have you checked out Fiverr and eLance to help you with your website?

_____

_____

_____

_____

_____

_____

_____

_____

Chapter 10
LET'S SOCIALIZE

"Inspiration is wonderful when it happens, but the writer must develop an approach for the rest of the time....The wait is simply too long."
—Leonard Bernstein

Building Relationships

If you are not familiar with blogging, it is time to learn. The best way to do this is to look at other author blogs that write similar books as yours. I often write blog posts from my own books and you can blog from your books as well. Just Google other authors using your genre and niche and see where they are. For instance, you bring up Google and type in your topic such as "author blogs about food." That will probably be too broad a topic, so then you narrow it to a particular food, like cookies or salads. Visit their websites and snoop around to see what they do. You could just jump in and comment on other blog posts, however, resist the urge to say, "Go to my blog and buy my book." This is a big no-no in the blogging world. Take it from someone who learned the ropes the hard way. If other bloggers see you as self-serving, they will block you or accuse you of spam. Blogging is all about building relationships, one post at a time. You might share your latest recipe for desert bars and tell other bloggers how much you value their opinion and invite them to post it on your blog. There is usually a place to add your own blog address when posting on other blogs.

Promote Your Blog

Add social media *share buttons* that show up after each blog post. The first thing I do the minute my blog post goes live is hit my share buttons! There are plenty of people from Fiverr who will be happy to set up your share buttons when they build your WordPress website. You want to promote your blog every chance you get and your social media channels are the place to do it. Do not try to sell anything on social media sites, just share your blog posts or announce book signings or Kindle Free Days. Anything you are giving away is a great promotional tool and it is acceptable to promote it on your social media accounts.

Pick Their Interest

If you get your website and blog up and running before your book is finished, that is great because you can begin promoting your book in advance of its launch.

Let's Socialize

Just be careful not to push people to buy your book in your postings. This would be a great time to post some tidbits about what to expect in your upcoming book. People are very curious about authors, so you might tell them a little about yourself and what prompted you to write on your particular topic. Post a picture of you so they can relate as you tell your stories. You can even post a picture of your cover, providing you have taken the initiative to get your cover done in advance of completing your book. If you have not completed your cover, this would be an excellent time to run a contest on your blog by having your contacts and subscribers vote on two or three cover choices. You can even do this with your book title. People love contests and you could offer a free chapter download from your upcoming book for those who participated. Some authors even offer a free Kindle for the prize. Be creative.

Connect the Dots

Your blog postings should be linked to all of your social media sites, like Twitter, Facebook, LinkedIn, YouTube, Goodreads, and Pinterest. People love photos when appropriate. I have a Barbara's Books Board for my Pinterest account and you can do the same. Pinterest now allows you to set your account up as a business account. That is if you have a business, and promoting and selling your books is definitely a business. If you do not have any social media accounts, I strongly urge you to get started ASAP! Any day you procrastinate is a day too long. The internet is not going to go away and it is the major player for author's to promote their work.

Give Them a Tweet

Another way to promote your new book is through Twitter at: www.twitter.com. Think of Twitter as micro-blogging. You only get 140 letters or numbers to create your post or mini blog. I used to go to Twitter and just sit there and stare, wondering what in the world can anyone accomplish tweeting 140 letters? I don't really care if your car broke down or your kid skipped school. How is that information going to help me sell my books? Well, it took me a few months before I finally jumped in and did my first tweet. I started tweeting short quotes from my own book. To my shock and amazement, people actually tweeted back and liked my quotes. I now have 3,350 Twitter followers. Go figure? Following is my Twitter address: http://www.twitter.com/barbarasmiller. Look me up, **Follow** me on Twitter, and send me a tweet!

Give Them a Freebie

When I did my book launch for "You Lost Your Marriage Not Your Life," I tweeted to my Twitter followers that my Kindle eBook would be offered free on Amazon for three days. There were 2,800 downloads of my free Kindle book and it drove my book to number one on Amazon in the divorce category. You are probably wondering why I would give my Kindle eBook away. Well, actually it is a means of promoting your book and getting it in the hands of readers. And after your promotion ends and your book ranks higher on Amazon, sales generally increase.

Amazon allows writers who list their eBook exclusively with Kindle Direct Publishing Select to have 5 free days within a 90 day period of time. You are not allowed to list your eBook anywhere else. Amazon is very strict about this rule, and if they catch you cheating, they simply won't pay you for eBook sales and may even delete your eBook from Amazon. However, this does not apply to any paperback or hard cover version of your book. Also, when you promote your eBook on your website, you can only show ten percent of your book. This would be similar to Amazon's *Look Inside This Book* feature, where you get a sneak preview of the book.

Let's Face It
Many of you are probably more familiar with Facebook, especially if you communicate with friends and family. This is a more friendly community to share about your book, but creating a Facebook Fan Page will be an even better place to share. Facebook only allows one account, but it recently launched the Facebook Fan Page for businesses. This is where you promote your books and book signings. You can create this page and still keep your Friends and Family page, although they each have the same login. You want to post content and get fans to Like you by clicking your Like button and hopefully leave comments. Facebook allows members to download a link on your WordPress author website or blog. This helps direct your website traffic to your Facebook Fan Page, but it also allows you to share your latest blog post.

What's In a Name
One word of caution; use your author name, because once you have created your profile on Twitter and Facebook, it is nearly impossible to change your user name. I use Barbara S. Miller or Barbara Miller Author, as there are several Barbara Miller's. When I first signed up for Facebook, the Facebook Fan Page did not exist, and like most people, I was trying to find friends and family, so I used my maiden name as a middle name. I now wish I would not have done that, but oh well, I now have to live with it. You can, however, have a different user name for your fan page, and I was able to use Barbara Miller Author. Facebook allowed me to use this as my login to my fan page because once you have enough traffic and content, Facebook allows you to incorporate your user name to create your own login to direct people to your fan page. My Facebook Fan Page url is: http://www.facebook.com/barbaramillerauthor

Let's Socialize

Please visit my Facebook Fan Page and **Like** me. If your author name is already taken, just try adding your middle initial or adding "author" like I did.

I See You

Always add your avatar or picture of you, not some caricature or animal. You want potential fans to know, like, and trust you. Facebook requires an email address to sign up and you will be using the same email on both Friends and Family and Facebook Fan Page accounts. Even though your friends and family will likely be supportive regarding promoting your book, if you do too much promoting on Friends and Family, Facebook might consider it spam. This is the reason they launched the Facebook Fan Page and this is where you want to do most of your promoting. Post a picture of your book and any other photos that relate to your writing. Grab a friend and go to your local book store with your book in hand and have her take a photo of you holding your book, and then post that photo on your website and Facebook Fan Page. Your Fan Page is not a place for a bunch of family photos; post those on your Friends and Family Page.

Express Yourself

It is always a good idea to search for writers with similar interest and check out their blogs. People love to have others comment on their blogs, as long as you are not constantly promoting yourself and your book. That is why it is called social media, and we want to get to know others instead of coming across as totally self-serving. Do your promoting on your fan page and drive traffic there by posting great content on your blog!

Let's Link Up

LinkedIn is another type of social media website, however, it was specifically designed to attract people in business. Once you set up your own website and publish your book, you are in business! Take advantage of LinkedIn and create your account. Post a photo of your book cover and describe your book in as much detail as possible. You will also fill out a detailed blurb on *About the Author*. Don't forget to fill in the how to contact you information. Make yourself shine! You never know what opportunities may be presented based on the subject of your book. There are vast numbers of blogs within LinkedIn. Do a search for other authors who write similar books as yours and check out their blog posts. They love having new members and welcome blog postings. Be careful not to promote on the blogs, just keep your profile up-to-date so others can see what you are about.

Make It a Good Read

Goodreads is now owned by Amazon and it is the largest site for readers of eBooks in the world. Take advantage of this opportunity to list your book on Goodreads. Fill out the necessary author profile and information about your book. You must do this as soon as your book is published. You can sponsor a contest and give away a certain number of books. This always sparks interest on Goodreads. Post your photo as well as one of the book cover. I hope you are now beginning to see the need for that professional photo of you, since it will be posted on every single social media channel. People will begin to recognize you and that is the first step. Goodreads also allows authors to post videos from your YouTube Channel, which might be your book trailer. Fill out everything you can about who you are and details about your book. Remember, help them to know, like, and trust you. When you run your Free Kindle Days, you will get several downloads from Goodreads! However, first they must know about you and your book. I cannot begin to express the value in getting your name and avatar out there.

Crying is all right in its way while it lasts. But you have to stop sooner or later, and then you still have to decide what to do."—
C. S. Lewis, *The Silver Chair*

Let's Socialize

Do you have a website or have someone who can help you build it?
_____
_____
_____
_____
_____
_____
_____
_____

Are you familiar with Facebook, Twitter, LinkedIn, YouTube, Goodreads, and Pinterest?
_____
_____
_____
_____
_____
_____
_____
_____

Have you started to create accounts on the above if you do not have them already?

_____

_____

_____

_____

_____

_____

_____

_____

Do you see why being connected to social media will help you promote your book?

_____

_____

_____

_____

_____

_____

_____

_____

Let's Socialize

Do you see that your book will not sell itself—it is up to you?

_____
_____
_____
_____
_____
_____
_____
_____

Have you listed various social media possibilities to get involved with?

_____
_____
_____
_____
_____
_____
_____
_____

Chapter 11
OKAY I'M IMMORTAL— NOW WHAT

"What really knocks me out is a book that, when you're all done reading it, you wish the author that wrote it was a terrific friend of yours and you could call him up on the phone whenever you felt like it. That doesn't happen much though."—J. D. Salinger

Congratulations

Well you just birthed your book, now you want to keep it alive and breathing. Let's start with a Press Release. Actually, three are ideal. PR Web is a popular company for authors, but it cannot be just about selling your book. They want it to read like someone wrote it other than you. You must write it in third person as an announcement about your book release and what it offers the reader. You are allowed to upload a book photo and an author photo. PR Web has strict guidelines to help you write the review.

It might seem a little overwhelming at first, but do not be intimidated. You can elect to hire Fiverr for this task or just Google other author's press releases. PR Web walks you through what will bring the best results. They are at http://www.prweb.com. Their Basic Package is $99.00 and they will try to upsell you to either their Standard Package for $149.00 or their Advanced Package for 249.00. I have used both the Basic Package and the Standard Package and had good results. If you intend to do three releases, start with PR Web, as you will then have your Press Release to use for the other two. I suggest PR Log as they are free. You can check them out at http://www.prlog.org and the other is Free Press Release at http://www.freepressrelease.com. I suggest the three releases to be launched a few days apart, as this will keep you active on Google and get your name and your book attention. When you rank high in Google searches, you may get calls for interviews, as the press release has your contact information and website.

Give It a Big Push

Reviews sell books and they are not easy to come by. I always order extra books and hand them out to friends and relatives in exchange for a review. Even then, most will not take the time to write a review, even when Amazon only requires twenty words minimum. This is sadly true, but remember when we discussed social media and those Kindle Free Days? Well, this is where it pays off. If you get enough free downloads, you are bound to get a few reviews.

Help Amazon Promote You

There is a feature Amazon offer that you would be remiss if you failed to take advantage of. It is your Author Page and you set it up through Author Central. Amazon actually encourages authors to post content on their personal page. All of your blog postings can be set up to post to your Author Page through what is called an RSS feed. Amazon tells you how to do it and it is easy. Not only that, but any book signings, publicity, videos, and book trailers can be posted or uploaded to your Author Page. Amazon suggests that you fill out your author profile in depth and take advantage of every word they allow. What makes this so valuable to you is that potential book buyers may visit this page to see what you are about. Amazon places a link at the bottom of your book listing to help potential buyers learn more about you. This is all **free** advertising! Amazon wants you to be successful and sell your books. The more books you sell, the more money you and Amazon both make. It's a win-win!

All Woven Together

Hopefully you have been able to see how this all becomes an interwoven plan of action and each plays off the other. For instance, Twitter will allow you to link to your Facebook page and when you post a promotional, it will automatically show up in your Facebook feed. You have to be careful with this, as at first I did not realize how it all worked, and if you remember those share buttons I suggested you add to your blog? I was sharing on Twitter and also on Facebook, so it was posted twice to Facebook. No big deal, except perhaps a little annoying to fans.

It is appropriate to tweet that you have just released your book, and you can add a link from Twitter right to your book on Amazon. Then go to your Facebook Fan Page and do the same thing, only here you will add your book cover and Press Release. When you finish your book and have it up on Amazon, just send me an email and your link and I will announce it to my Twitter followers.

Give Them a High Five

Let's not forget Fiverr at this point, as they have special gigs for promoting your book. They will blast it to their Twitter followers for five bucks. This works best for your Kindle Free Days.

Give It a Spin

Remember I mentioned earlier that we would talk about *Spinoffs* and how they can increase your bottom line? Well, video is the darling of social media at this point. I know you are wondering how many times I am going to hammer on this issue, but here it goes one more time, "They need to know, like, and trust you!" What better way to accomplish this than a video of you describing why you wrote your book? You can upload it to YouTube and have something on that new channel you just created. Once it is on YouTube, you can put it on your own website, as well as your author page on Amazon. You can put it on Facebook and also put a link on Twitter. Don't forget LinkedIn and Goodreads. You are not selling anything, you are simply connecting with your fans! You can create a link directly to your book on Amazon. Just resist saying, "Go to Amazon and buy my book!" They already know you want them to buy your book, but you are only chatting on your video as to why you decided to write this particular book.

Tell the World Your Story

Public speaking puts terror in many hearts, but nobody knows your story better than you, so stand up and tell it! If you become ill at the thought of getting up in public, try joining Dale Carnegie or your local Toast Master's Club. There are wonderful people there who help members get over the fear of public speaking. You may already belong to a local club who would love to hear your story. The Chamber of Commerce is a great place to network as well as a Rotary Club, Kiwanis Club, Book Clubs, and your local library. You will find opportunities everywhere just waiting to hear your story, and don't forget your church.

Don't forget to do what I did and pay a visit to your local bookstore. I took my book in and gave it to the woman in charge of local authors and book-signings. She took my book and much to my surprise, I received an email stating that she had ordered copies of my book for the Self-help section of the book store.

Post Regularly to Your Blog

Even though you want to keep your name out there, let's not overdo it. People want to hear your story, but not every day. Blog starting out about two times a month. Once a week is okay, but when you are new, you may run out of material. I get emails frequently from online gurus and marketers and it is exhausting trying to keep up with everything. Just blog excerpts from your book or related issues that your fans will find interesting. Comment on other blogs with similar interest. Most importantly, have fun!

Okay I'm Immortal—Now What

I am so happy that you have purchased and read my book. I sincerely hope you will use this book as a guide to help you get started on writing your book! If you already have a manuscript that is hiding in a drawer or stored on your computer, it is time to breathe new life into it. Amazon makes writing and publishing books easy, so let's do it. The world needs our stories!

"All good books are alike in that they are truer than if they had really happened and after you are finished reading one you will feel that all that happened to you and afterwards it all belongs to you: the good and the bad, the ecstasy, the remorse and sorrow, the people and the places and how the weather was."—Ernest Hemingway

Do you see how Press Releases sell books and up your ranking on Google?

_____

_____

_____

_____

_____

_____

_____

_____

Have you researched book reviews and their value to authors?

_____

_____

_____

_____

_____

_____

_____

_____

Do you see the value for using Kindle Free Days as a great way to launch your book?

_____
_____
_____
_____
_____
_____
_____
_____

How could you use Social Media for your own private advertising campaign?

_____
_____
_____
_____
_____
_____
_____
_____

Are you prepared to learn as much as possible about promoting your book?

Have you noticed the share and like buttons others are using on social media sites? Do you see how they could be useful to promote your book?

Okay I'm Immortal—Now What

"You can sit there, tense and worried, freezing the creative energies, or you can start writing something. It doesn't matter what. In five or ten minutes, the imagination will heat, the tightness will fade, and a certain spirit and rhythm will take over."
—Leonard Bernstein

About Barbara

Barbara Miller, author, motivational speaker, and certified master life coach, is the founder of Barbara & Company International, Inc. Barbara studied Health & Wellness at Ashford University and also studied at Kendall College of Art & Design. Barbara earned her master life coaching certification through American University of NLP.

Barbara is the author of, *Dancing in Rhythm with the Universe, 10 Steps to Choreographing Your Best Life,* and *You Lost Your Marriage Not Your Life, How to Create the Life You Want Your Way,* and her newly released book, *How to write a Book, Easy Steps to Write, Publish, and Promote Your Book.*

Barbara's main goal is to empower her readers to lead their best life yet by creating balance mentally, physically, social-emotionally, and spiritually. She resides in Naples, Florida with her husband David.

About Barbara

I sincerely want to thank you for purchasing and reading my book. I am pleased to offer a special bonus to you as a thank you for opting-in to my monthly newsletter. For my new coaching clients, I offer a free one-half hour coaching session, but I would like to offer you a **one hour free session** to discuss your goals. This is a $150.00 value. You may email me at:
barbara@barbaraandcompany.com

http://www.princessdiaryblog.com
http://www.barbaraandcompany.com
barbara@barbaraandcompany.com
http://www.twitter.com/barbarasmiller
http://www.facebook.com/barbaramillerauthor
http://www.youtube.com/BARBARASMIL

www.ingramcontent.com/pod-product-compliance
Lightning Source LLC
Chambersburg PA
CBHW080521110426
42742CB00017B/3198